DESIGNING
ECOMMERCE
WEBSITES

OVER 50 UX DESIGN TIPS & TRICKS
FOR GREAT ONLINE SHOPS

TRANSMITTER PRESS

First published in Great Britain in 2017 by
Transmitter Press
Copyright © Matt Isherwood 2017

ISBN 978-0-9957313-1-8

ABOUT THE AUTHOR

Matt Isherwood is a UX consultant who helps ecommerce sites improve their design via qualitative and quantitative data. He specialises in working with growing start-ups. He started his career at the BBC, before being the lead UX designer at onefinestay, and has taught workshops and courses at General Assembly.

96 **CHECKOUT**   124 **MORE**

So, you're working on an ecommerce website? Whether it's your own site or you're designing or developing for someone else, this book should be able to help. It contains advice you can apply to get the core user experience working smoothly.

One ecommerce website that I worked on (I won't name them) illustrates what this book aims to solve. Like most of my projects, I first set up user testing to see what users thought of the site. Their product was great and the visual design and imagery were beautiful. Users were immediately impressed and said how excited they were.

However the search filters were a bit fiddly, the product page wasn't clearly laid out, and when it came to making a purchase, users got stuck. They weren't sure how the product was priced or how to select dates. And if they did work this out it then wasn't clear how to change things, so they'd have to start all over again. The initial great impression had worn off.

It didn't matter that they had the best-looking product in the world, with the sharpest type and colour combinations, as they were tripping up on the essential functions. Many times I've seen an experience most defined by the frustration of things not working as people expect. Of course there's room to innovate and delight but doing so without a working funnel underneath only makes things worse.

Who this is for

This book has been designed to work for a wide-range of people who sell online. It is applicable to any site that follows the ecommerce funnel—regardless of the sector you work in.

My aim is that this book works for more than just designers as there are plenty of roles that influence the design process. I've tried to avoid technical jargon and requiring too much prior knowledge, so the likes of marketers, developers, and startup CEOs can dip in and out. If there's anything you don't understand, I've put a glossary at the back.

This book gives advice that is device-agnostic and can apply on desktop, tablet, and mobile (I make clear where it doesn't apply to a device). Ecommerce websites tend to attract a high number of mobile users so the modern website must be responsive and work for a broad range of mobile screen sizes.

Why listen to me?

I'm a UX designer with over eight years experience and over five of them in the ecommerce space. I've worked with a range of different size companies who have sold a variety of products. This includes three and a half years at a high-growth travel company (onefinestay) and two years of freelance consulting to startups. All of the advice in this book has been learned from these real engagements and I now apply them when I come to design.

I've taught on this subject for over three years too. I've developed a lot of the advice in this book through teaching regular workshops at General Assembly in London where it's proven to be robust and applicable to a wide variety of people. I've also written pretty solidly for the last two years, with weekly blogs on UX design as well as putting together my two ebooks (one on Data-Driven UX Design and one on iPhone app usability).

You should be wary of people offering 'best practice' so I bring you this content as advice rather than guaranteed fact. But this is advice gained working at the sharp end of ecommerce UX design across multiple websites. It's what I've learned over the course of my career and it's what people hire me for as a UX consultant. They hire me because I've designed ecommerce sites before before; I've researched many websites in this space; I've looked at a lot of analytics; I've analysed many user tests; and not to mention I've shopped on plenty myself.

The ecommerce funnel—how this book is structured

This book mirrors the structure that the vast majority of ecommerce websites use. These pages don't just exist due to convention and user expectation but because they solve jobs a user needs to do when they shop. It's known as a funnel because there are always more people at the top who taper off to the few that purchase at the bottom (see image on **page 11**).

Landing

The landing pages are the equivalent of the shop window in a physical store and the job here is to show users what the site offers and encourage them to 'enter the store'. The tips here will look at how you can get that message across quickly and get people to click further.

LANDING

SEARCH

PRODUCT

CHECKOUT

MORE

Search

This is similar to the inside layout of the store and the job here is to help users compare different options to find something they want to buy. These tips cover both the structure of the search page itself and what should live on the search result listings.

Product

The product pages do the job of a product's packaging in a real-life store. It needs to show off the thing despite you not being able to see it. It also must convey all the details and information you need to know to be confident in making a purchase. These tips take you through what you need to have on a product page for it to be a success.

Checkout

This is where the user comes to pay and often organise delivery. It's a somewhat standardised process so there are conventions to learn but also things you can do to make it convenient for the user to give you their money. This advice will help you make this process a smooth one.

More

Finally there's a section for hints and tips that don't fit in the ecommerce flow. These include principles that apply to the website as a whole and a few other pages worth mentioning that can help users access the ecommerce funnel.

Not all sites will require every step of the funnel. For example, if you're selling a single product then it's possible to just have a product page without landing or search. And if you're only selling a few products you probably don't need the search functionality. But as all sites grow they do end up requiring all four of these steps.

Each tip is presented on a double-page spread, where possible with an illustration to help clarify the meaning. These illustrations are deliberately kept in an outline, wireframe style as the point isn't to give you things to copy but concepts to think about. The illustrations aren't based on any particular size or dimensions of device.

This book is designed so you can easily dip in and out, for whatever need you have at the time. I wanted to make this as easy to pick up and use as possible and not a theoretical tome.

I hope it will act as a starting point to help you but don't see it as the be all and end all. Not every piece of advice will apply to every site so please build on it if you learn more, and always experiment and test with your own site.

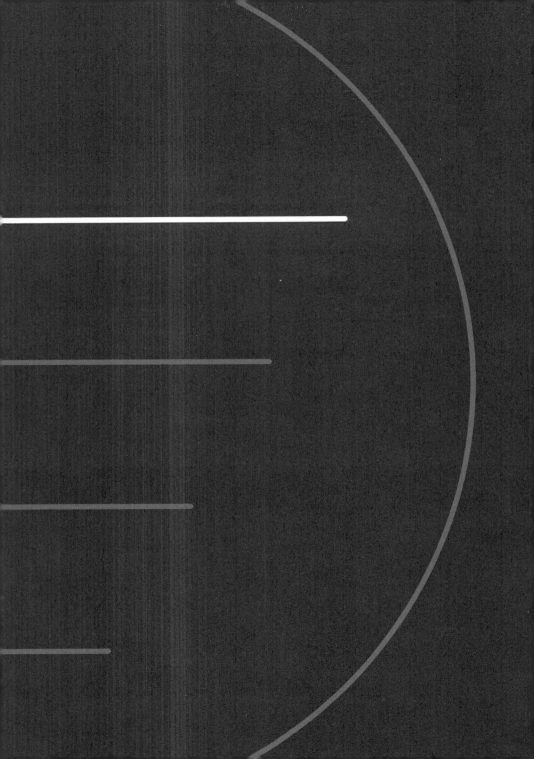

LANDING

Technically any page can be a landing page, as it can simply describe the location that people enter the site at. However for this book I mean a page specifically designed for a user's introductory experience. A good site thinks about where the users are coming from and presents them with a page that recognises they will have a few key questions that need answering.

Every site has a homepage and in the early days of a website this will be the dominant landing page for the majority of users. As sites grow and marketing effort intensifies it becomes important to have specific landing pages for certain campaigns. This is particularly important for paid search where the page and headings need to match the keywords that people have been searching for, or they won't think it is relevant for their needs.

Whether it's a homepage or a campaign landing page it represents the top of your funnel and there are certain things it needs to do. In retail terms it's your shop window and often the first impression people have of your website and company. You need to tell people what you offer and why you're different and you need to do it quickly. New users are quick to bounce if they don't see the benefit of what you offer: very few people have the patience to hang around.

You also need to show and prove to your users that you are of a sufficient quality to be trusted. And then give users a clear onward step to get 'into the shop' and see the products you have on offer. Landing pages should have a very clear metric for success. They succeed by pushing people through the site, usually onto search, so this is the conversion rate to watch. Pretty much any other metric is a distraction. A low bounce rate is good for a landing page as you don't want users leaving but the most important thing is that users go to the next step in your funnel.

Having a clarity of purpose makes designing easier as everything you do can be measured against a goal. A lot of this section of the book is related to the concept of attention ratio—an ideal page should have a ratio of 1:1 (one page with one link to the goal). Practical considerations mean you'll probably need a few more links, but the aim should be to keep that ratio as close to 1:1 as possible. If you're getting to a ratio of 30:1 or 40:1 then there should be big room for improvement.

These tips will help delve into how you can focus your users attention and get those clicks (or taps) in the direction you want.

SHOW WHAT YOU SELL

The first thing users need to understand when they come through your door is what you sell. Sounds obvious but it is essential as when a user lands they want to know they are in the right place. Start them off feeling unclear and they either leave or you're fighting to turn it around in the rest of the journey.

The best and quickest way to do this is through your imagery—be it photography, video, or illustrations. Humans are visual creatures so this is the information we process fastest, plus there's a lot of detail you can include in an image. Obviously imagery focused on the product you sell, for example a piece of furniture, gets this message across but you can go further.

There are lots of expectations coded into every image: are you using the right ones for your site? If a site has an image of a middle-aged woman attending a classy event in a city then you instantly understand the intended gender, age, location, and income demographics of the target audience. If the woman looks like a model and the photography is high quality then you'd recognise these as tropes of fashion. If a coffee brand has a photo of a man in his 20s with a beard, sat at a rustic-looking cafe, you would see this as one for urban hipsters.

The main explanation can be done via the imagery, leaving the words to explain things that are less obvious (see **page 20**).

"THIS *IS* *THE* INFORMATION *WE* PROCESS FASTEST"

SPELL OUT HOW YOU ARE DIFFERENT

If the first thing users need to understand when they arrive is what you do, then the second is how you are different to everybody else. What you do can be shown through imagery and design choices that suggest a target audience. How you are different usually means stating it very clearly.

Explaining quickly how you are different is very important because otherwise what reason do people have to stay on your site? Why not just go to Amazon, eBay, Booking.com or another big aggregator where they've already got an account? Your difference should be something that marks you out as special and shouldn't be something that others can easily offer. Priding yourself on free shipping and free returns isn't special but now increasingly common.

Your difference should be a unique selling point and ideally focused on just one thing. Don't muddy the waters and present three or four things. Once you've got it worked out, you should be able to say this thing in only a few words and you should tell users straight away (probably above the fold). Good examples can be niches ("we're the only people specialising in this thing") or special services ("free personalisation of products") or in how the product/service is produced ("no sweats shops, eco-friendly etc").

Be careful not to get too clever in your wording so you leave people guessing how you differ: inventing words, using hashtags, and using jargon can all lead to this kind of confusion.

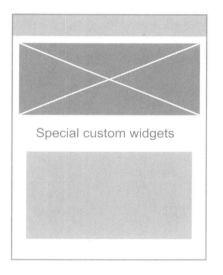

Special custom widgets

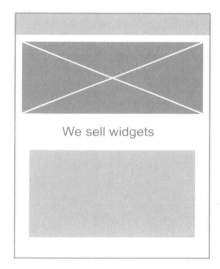

We sell widgets

DON'T HIDE INFORMATION IN CAROUSELS

Carousels are a common feature of ecommerce websites and there are some out there who will seek to tell you that they are a terrible idea. I'm not one of those people: they can be a good idea, but only if used correctly. Cramming them with too much information and copy is the wrong approach.

The best way to think of carousels is like mini videos. The slides should auto-play as very few users will bother to click through them manually. Think about how the content works together to show what you offer. If you're selling something that isn't easily explained in one image, then a few can combine to show things more clearly. A service that offers lots of different places for people to stay is better shown in a few images rather than a single one.

What you shouldn't do is have your carousel populated with slides containing lots of text or offers that compete with each other. I've seen this happen a lot on department store sites where they want to push a multitude of sales and offers. An excess of information can leave users paralysed by choice and the clicks on that third or fourth slide are going to be tiny. As for a number of slides, four is probably enough—any more and they're going to be missed as users scroll past.

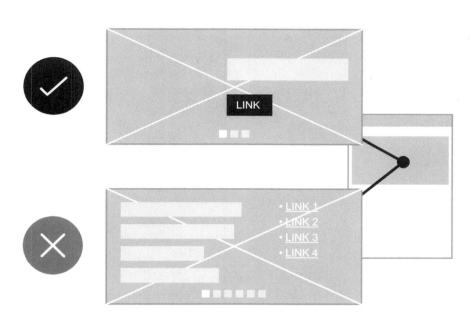

LINK

• LINK 1
• LINK 2
• LINK 3
• LINK 4

A CLEAR BUTTON TO START SHOPPING

Every webpage should have a primary action it wants users to take. A homepage or landing page has the very clear purpose of getting users to take the next step in buying, which usually means searching for products.

There should be an obvious link or button which takes users to search. It should be presented in a contrasting colour that is barely used elsewhere on the site to help it stand out.

It could be just a simple link to all the products in your store or if the user needs to enter parameters for their search (such as location and dates in a travel site) it can be part of a module with the relevant fields. Either way, the button should be marked out by a strong colour and it should be obvious what it does with a sensible action word like 'shop' or 'search'.

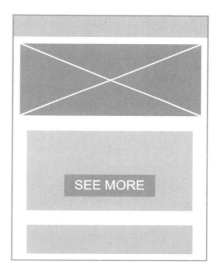

PRESS AND LOGOS HELP LEGITIMISE

Don't underestimate the usefulness of recognisable brand names or press logos to help reassure users that you are a decent company. It may feel like the oldest sales technique in the book but time and again I've watched user tests where people express how much more trust they feel in the brand when they see them.

If you've been lucky enough or worked hard to get good press coverage then don't forget to show users these quotes and publication logos early on. It might just make the difference between whether they give you more attention or go back to a site they've used before.

If you don't have much in the way of press coverage, it's certainly worth looking into getting some. Or you can use review services like TripAdvisor or TrustPilot which plenty of users recognise and put faith in. Whatever you do, don't make it up or bend quotes into looking like positive coverage. As well as being unethical it only takes one person to work this out and expose you, potentially spreading it all over social media.

"This product really delivers top quality"

Techblog.com

"This is the best thing made ever, you should own it!"

The Bible

TELL A STORY, DON'T PUSH ADS

The elements on your landing page should be working together to help users understand what is being offered. Each section should answer different questions users will have about the site rather than having lots of disparate bits shouting for your attention.

For example, you might start the page with a module showing what you do, and follow it with a way to continue the buying journey, then press & testimonials, more on the key differences of the brand, and finally some general company 'about' information. Avoid sections that alternate between repeated CTAs to shop or search and big brand promises that look like adverts.

Having content that looks like banner adverts and 'shouts' at users to visit their bit of the site can be counter-productive as users are well attuned to ignoring this kind of thing. Now you have the user on your site, you can be more relaxed and help the user explore rather than compete for their interest.

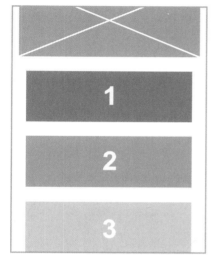

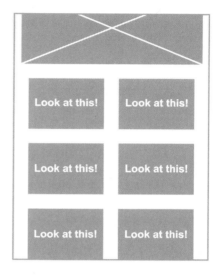

DON'T REPEAT LINKS

Following on from the last point, many websites have a common problem where the same link ends up competing against itself. For example, if you've decided that your most important link is to send people to search, it can be very tempting to have this on the page multiple times. You might think this means they are less likely to miss it.

However, with every extra link you're creating more things for the users to take in and understand—each repeated link increases the complexity of your page. On top of this, if there are lots of similar links on the page then the user is going to wonder which is the 'right' one or the one they should visit first. If there's a search link at the top, middle, and bottom of the page, they're only going to pick one but could be left wondering if they should have gone elsewhere.

I understand the temptation to try and increase click-throughs but you're much better off simplifying your homepage and constructing a very clear primary CTA, that they can't miss.

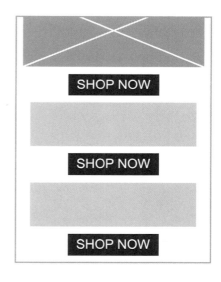

BIG STORES SHOULDN'T SHOW PRODUCTS

One question that comes up a lot when designing ecommerce sites is whether or not to put products on the homepage. Managers or merchandising folk are often keen to get products on there that they want to push, in the belief it will drive users through to these pages and increase sales. Unfortunately this isn't often the case and for big sites this can be a premature time to do it.

If you're a site with hundreds of products then what are the chances the user landing on your page will immediately want the three to six products you've put there? Pretty low. In fact you could be confusing them into thinking this is all you offer, or you may end up with a few products that aren't representative of your store offering. Even if they do click through, they may not like the product and can exit without having seen the full range of options available. If you're big you should show the categories of products on the home page to give an overview of the full range you offer. And you should be aiming to drive users through to search.

For small sites (with fewer than ten products) it's fine to show products on your homepage. After all, categories are going to be overkill and these few products *are* your offering. Allow users to quickly get a sense of what they can buy and can click through to do it.

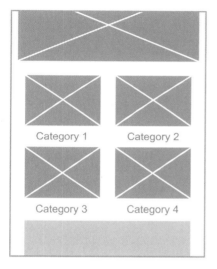

Category 1   Category 2

Category 3   Category 4

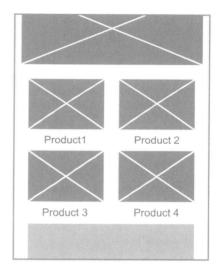

Product1   Product 2

Product 3   Product 4

DON'T MAKE IT TOO LONG

It can be highly tempting to keep going with your landing page, as once you've got the user on there, you want to tell them everything. But the longer you make it the more you risk the user switching off. Whilst users do scroll and keeping things above the fold shouldn't be an overarching priority, I've seen the content near the bottom of long landing pages get completely skipped in user tests.

A good model to follow is to make sure you cover these sections of information:

— The brand and USP
— Search CTA
— Social proof
— About the products or company

And stop once you've shown this. Remember that the more links you put on the page, the more distractions you're giving the user from your main CTA and the key thing you really want them to do. If you have lots of nuance to explain don't throw it all at your users straight away, consider progressively revealing it through the funnel.

"THE LONGER YOU MAKE IT THE MORE YOU RISK THE USER SWITCHING OFF"

CAREFUL WITH POP-UPS

There's often a great temptation to get users' email addresses as soon as possible. It can be expensive to acquire users so you obviously want to capture as many as you can to market to them again over email, which tends to have a high conversion rate. However there are things you need to think about before blitzing the user with pop-ups and sign-up fields.

Do they understand the site? Have you given them enough time to take a look at your message and what you sell and for them to decide if they're interested? If you're popping the message up as soon as they land, the chances are they don't know much about you yet and will immediately dismiss it.

Are you offering something of value? Requesting an email address requires a value exchange: if you want something of theirs, you've got to offer something in return. In my experience, real cash discounts or decent percentage discounts (greater than 10%) tend to get noticed. Just promising 'updates and latest offers' doesn't.

Are they a user worth having? You may work out a way to gather lots of user email addresses via your landing pop-ups but will these users ever open your emails? Are they just the type that are highly price sensitive, so use the discount and then move on? I've seen a lot of users have specific spam email addresses for signing up to offers. You'll find lots of data out there on people who have increased email sign ups on their site, but very few will tell you how good those users were and whether they converted, so think before rushing to implement it.

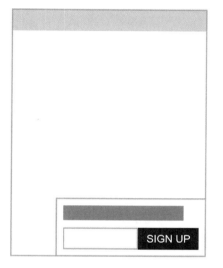

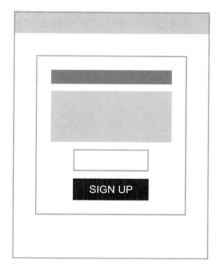

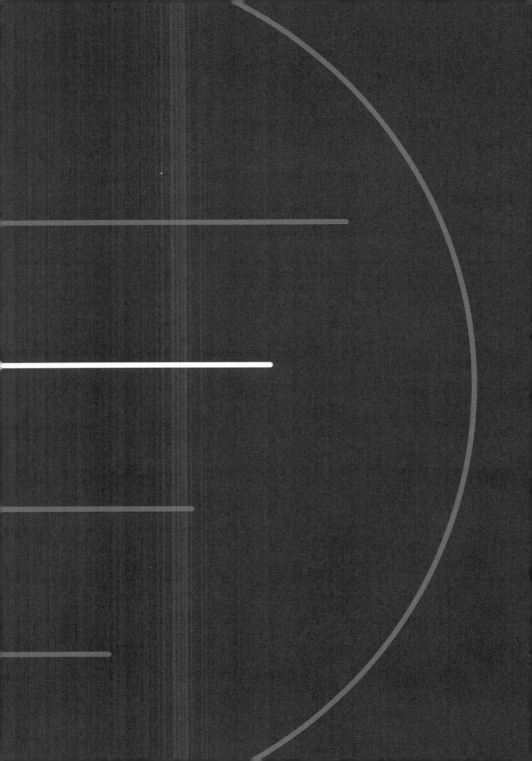

SEARCH

The search section is sometimes referred to as 'category' pages, as this is where products are displayed by category. It can also be called 'browse' on websites where 'search' is reserved for users typing a specific query. But generally I've found 'search' is the most universal term, as the user's task involves sifting through options via a set of filters to find something.

If you've got your users through to this point then they should understand who you are and should be interested in what you're selling. Now they want to see what the actual options are. They will use this page to get a sense of the products you sell by judging them en masse, for example seeing the range of prices available. They will also look at products individually and understand how they differ.

Search can be split into two parts, both covered in this chapter:

— First we cover the structure of the page itself, and how the different elements can help the user find things. The search stage of the funnel is about helping users find the right product, and as humans we're limited in how much information we can store in our head at any one time. If your site is small (with around 10-20 products) then you may not need some of the structural elements like filters, but they become more important the bigger a website gets.

— Secondly we look at the individual search results and the components you require to give users everything they need to make a decision. Even if you don't need filters you will need to present your products in a way that is easy to compare. There are some essential pieces of information you should almost certainly have about each product.

How your search page looks will vary depending on what you're selling and who your audience are. Are you selling something that is expensive, featuring locations or impressive detail? Then your photography will be an important part of your offering—make this a bigger element to excite the user. Contrast this to a site selling something more practical like cleaning products. In this case what it looks like doesn't matter but how it performs does, making it a more rational purchasing decision. Here you should emphasise the product data.

Whilst we can be fairly certain about the core components of a good search page, you should also have a sense of how your users think and what motivates them towards making purchases. If your user testing shows that they regularly jump between search and product pages to find a detail, then that piece of information could be displayed at the search level. These details are often things that only matter to your audience and the product you're selling.

Consider the search section to be a shop floor: think about how you lay it out for easy navigation so that users are encouraged to spend time browsing.

VERTICAL NOT HORIZONTAL FILTERS

In the design challenge of finding room on your search pages it can be very tempting to put your filters horizontally across the top of the page. After all, it creates width and allows more focus on the products themselves. However this then means your filters become very space-limited and users can easily scroll past this area. If a user misses the filters and you have lots of products then they're more likely to see mostly irrelevant items, which is a poor experience.

I'd recommend running your filters vertically down the left side of your page. This is an established pattern that has worked for a long time and most users understand it. I've watched many user tests where users are happy going through large numbers of filter options when listed vertically, and they have the advantage of being able to see results alongside. Do make sure the search results dynamically update with every filter selection and there isn't a 'search' button they need to click, or you're doubling the work.

On mobile of course you're not going to have the space for this. Instead it will require a tap to bring up most of the filters (and you can expect fewer people to view/adjust them as a result) but you can have the same filters stack vertically and slide in from the side, maintaining consistency.

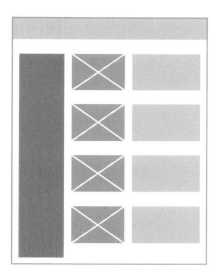

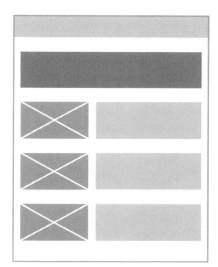

HIDDEN FILTERS DON'T GET FOUND

Once you have a large number of products on your site, you increase the amount of data to potentially search by, often requiring more filters. It can then be tempting to hide some filters behind 'advanced' links or 'more filters' buttons.

However, you should be very aware that the vast majority of users are never going to bother looking here. I've worked on sites that hide some filters and the analytics data showed less than 1% of users click them. This can be for a variety of reasons: it is perceived as too much extra work; they don't know what they'll find there; or they expect the most useful ones to be shown by default.

This isn't to say that you may not have good reasons for hiding some filters, but just expect that they won't be seen by most people. You're making an active decision when you show and hide things and the power of the default option is very strong. It is worth asking yourself whether a filter is needed at all if it is going to get so little use.

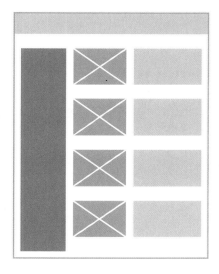

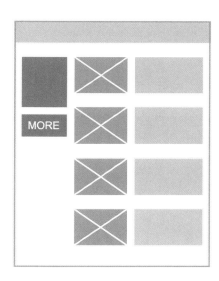

SEARCH FIELDS SHOULD AUTO-COMPLETE

If you're going to offer a search field for users to type into, it has to help out the user. The biggest danger of using free text search is that once you have it people can type pretty much anything in there (and they will). This can result in lots of null results screens, which is a frustrating experience for the user. To prevent this your search field must incorporate auto-complete and auto-suggest.

Auto-complete is when the field shows search terms that could be formed from the letters the user has started to type. This is particularly useful when you sell a limited set of things and you need to guide users to the right search terms.

Auto-suggest is when the field gives the user similar searches to the terms they have entered, or searches that are popular on the site. You can also suggest individual products in order to direct the user straight to those product pages and help speed up the searching process. Between these options you can guide the user away from dead-end searches and also help educate them about the kind of products you sell.

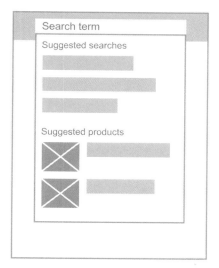

Search term

Suggested searches

Suggested products

Search term

SAVE PREFERENCES

If a user logs in or creates an account during their journey, then you should save their search filters or preferences, to help make future visits quicker. It will help your brand feel so much easier and less hassle than going elsewhere.

If they're searching for clothing, their size preference is unlikely to change (you can also default to this size on product pages when displaying stock levels). If they're looking for accommodation, the number of people on their trip is probably going to remain constant. If they're specifying dates for an event, their availability is likely to be similar to the last time they looked.

You can store these as preferences in their account or simply by pre-filling fields with what they last entered. The simple act of starting with a smart default rather than nothing will often help them save a bit of time. They can always change it for the occasions where they're looking for something different.

"HELP YOUR BRAND FEEL EASIER AND LESS HASSLE THAN GOING ELSEWHERE"

EXPLAIN THE CATEGORY

Search pages are often very similar or even the same as category pages. Category pages are used as a scoped set of search results focussing on one product line. If we take the example of jewellery, a category could be broad like 'rings', more specific like 'diamond rings', or it could be a branded range such as 'Classic Collection Rings'.

The more specific the category, the more it is going to need some kind of explanation to the user. You need to help them understand what they're looking at and why it's different and of interest to them. A bit like the first copy they see on a landing page, users should be able to quickly 'get' the category and if it's right for them.

Whilst a high-level introduction is a necessity, some products might require more explanation. Don't do this on the category page itself as this is a place to view and compare products. Instead link off to an information page (see **page 130**) with more detail and copy about the product line, where you can take the time to explain more to the user. At the bottom of this page should be a clear CTA to get back to the ecommerce funnel.

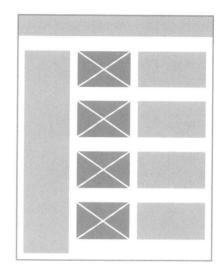

THE RIGHT NUMBER ON THE MAP

If you're dealing with selling properties or holiday accommodation then a map is an important element of your search page. Almost all users will want to get to grips with where something is before deciding whether to pay for it.

There are no fixed answers for how to arrange your map as it will depend on the size of area you're covering and how many results you have to show. It is always important to not overwhelm the user with too many results and considering the following will help you do that:

— What zoom level will you set the map to initially? Ideally you want to have as many of your results as possible showing but this could vary from place to place.
— How much do you want the user to be able to zoom? Does it make sense for them to zoom all the way into the map or all the way out to country-level? Probably not, so you might want to limit this.
— Are you going to group the results? One way to deal with lots of results is to group them into areas, creating a larger icon showing the number of results in that area. This makes sense if you have lots of results but only if the area groupings are understood by users.
— Are you going to limit the number of results on screen at any one time? Another way to tackle lots of results is only to show a handful at once (often relating to how many are visible in a list view next to the map). If you do this then it needs to be clear to the user that more results are available by moving the map or changing search parameters.

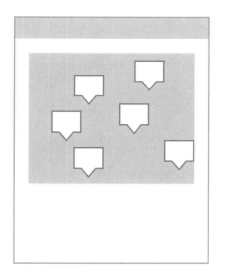

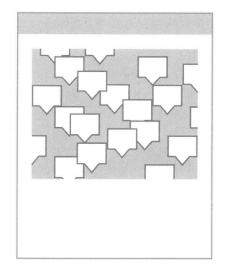

A FINDER TO CUT
THROUGH COMPLEXITY

Maybe a traditional search isn't the best approach for your site. Maybe the products you sell are specific and the user needs to buy exactly the right thing or it won't be compatible with their needs. If the user needs guidance to reach the right outcome then perhaps you should add a finder tool to your search.

A finder would usually sit alongside search, although in some cases it could replace it altogether. The idea would be that it helps guide the user step-by-step through the buying process. It would ask users questions about their needs, getting them to make a decision at each step, before presenting them with results that match their exact requirements.

This is a great way to show expertise in an area and gain trust from users, especially if it's an item that users don't buy very often, causing them to feel uncertain shopping in your category. It could also be something that makes sense to implement if you are seeing a lot of products being returned because users are ordering the wrong size or wrong item altogether.

  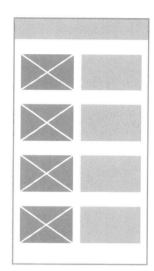

1 **2** **3**

HAVE DISTINCT TITLES

It's obvious that your items need a title for the user to know what they're looking at. It's less obvious to know what makes for a good title. There are a few rules I like to follow for strong, memorable titles:

— Keep them fairly short (four words maximum) or people will never be able to recall them later.
— Make them unique—really generic titles are going to make it hard for the user to find it again ('classic t-shirt' in a site with 100s of t-shirts for example). Instead add a bit of personality with a name you won't find repeated elsewhere.
— If they're going to be very different, like the funky sounding IKEA product names, then add the product type next to it, e.g. 'Ektorp | Armchair'.
— Don't cram the titles with SEO information or product details, as much as marketing folk might want you to. Things like size and colour should be found in their relevant place on the page for comparison, and shouldn't need to be hunted for within the title.

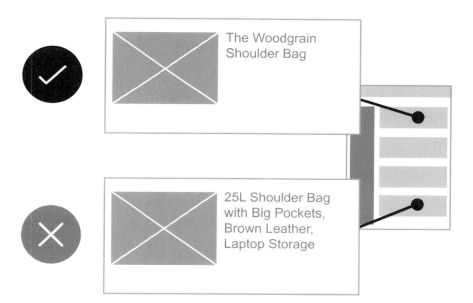

The Woodgrain Shoulder Bag

25L Shoulder Bag with Big Pockets, Brown Leather, Laptop Storage

NAMING CONNOTATIONS AREN'T ALWAYS UNDERSTOOD

Product names alter perceptions. Very few ecommerce sites have such strong brands that users will be willing to learn a new language to understand what you're trying to sell.

I've worked on a few ecommerce sites where the names were opaque and didn't mean anything to the users. In the user tests people completely ignored content that would have been right for them because they didn't want to risk clicking on something they didn't understand. This advice applies to including all sorts of things in your titles, such as technical terms, famous people, historic events, or specific location names.

For example if you're offering a party experience for young people, err towards calling it something descriptive like 'Cocktails and Clubs' rather than the more obscure 'Manhattan Meltdown' or 'Cosmopolitan Class'. Ambiguous wording means the user has to fill in the blanks and unless you've put a lot of effort into marketing your uniquely named things, it can cause them to interpret your products incorrectly.

Another example, if you're selling a trip in London called 'Brixton Food Tour', very few people other than locals would know it features exciting worldwide street food and boutique restaurants. Nationally the area is still more synonymous with 80s riots and internationally it would probably mean nothing. Connotations take a long time to change.

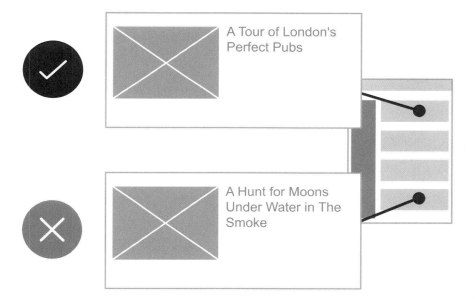

A Tour of London's Perfect Pubs

A Hunt for Moons Under Water in The Smoke

PRICE FOR COMPARISON

The price should be present on your search listings, as it's a vital piece of information. It's a huge driver in how people choose what to look at, and being able to sort and filter by price is a frequently used tool. It should be clear and it should be referring to the same thing on each product.

Some products require a more comparable price such as price per unit when buying in bulk or price per 100ml/100g when dealing with food. I implemented a price per room on a holiday rental site, to better help the user compare across different size properties and to compare against hotel room prices. Comparison is the name of the game here, and people won't be able to find the deals they're after if they're not comparing the same thing.

You should avoid the use of 'from' prices as it doesn't give the user much to go on—just how high does it go above that 'from' price? The exception to this is if you can't show an accurate price without information from the user: for example they need to specify dates for a trip.

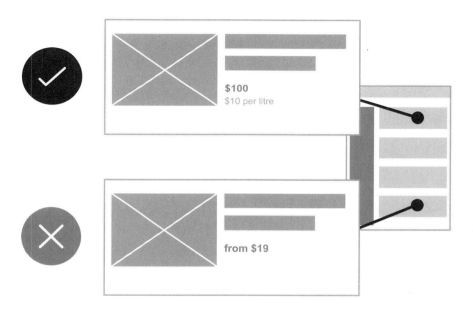

$100
$10 per litre

from $19

IMAGES MATTER

Even on the search page, where images can often just be small thumbnails of the product for sale, they are important to the user. They are obviously another key part of helping the user make a decision about which product to select. In fact in many cases the image tells you a lot more than any text can. If you're selling things like clothing, furniture, or properties then they rely on the user making a subjective choice between the different options.

I've worked on sites where the images on search haven't just been a small visual differentiator but something to be shown off at a large size. I've then seen users react very positively to this (it doesn't matter where they are on the site, great photography is always loved).

It can be hard to summarise some products in a single image, particularly experiential ones or locations. So if you think something can be better sold in a few images then do so. It's becoming increasingly common to see multiple photos in search thumbnails with a subtle arrow to scroll through them. Some clothing sites are helped by offering the option of seeing just the product or it being worn by a model. Bear in mind you can't just offer multiple images on some products or users will get frustrated when they aren't there on others.

The only time when images don't make much sense to be big, is when they are for products where how they look is unimportant. For example, with electronic components or computer parts it's much more important what the stats and figures say, as how they look is pretty interchangeable.

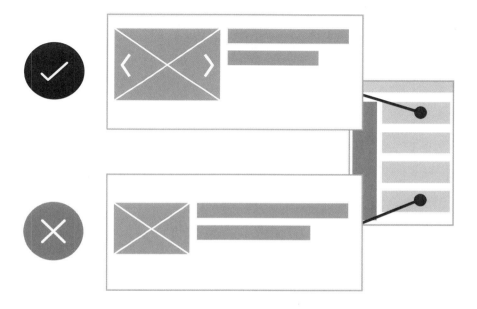

RATINGS FOR GUIDANCE

If you do collect ratings and reviews on your products and you have a decent number of them per product, you should probably show them to your users on the search page. This applies less to luxury products which aim to be unique and not seen as interchangeable.

Ratings are particularly important if you are selling products that people don't buy very often or are technical in nature. For example, users are likely to buy a television once every 5-10 years but are unlikely to be up to speed with the latest technical specifications. Here user ratings become a very helpful way of sifting through the content to find the good stuff. Experiences that users may only do once, like visit a hotel or restaurant, also require other people's knowledge to help them make a decision (hence the importance of TripAdvisor).

If you show a rating then there are two things you must do. The first is to show the total the score is out of—either visually (often with stars) or in words. The second is to show how many people have reviewed the product in total to show how meaningful that score is, e.g. 200 people giving a score of 4.5 is more useful than two people giving a score of five.

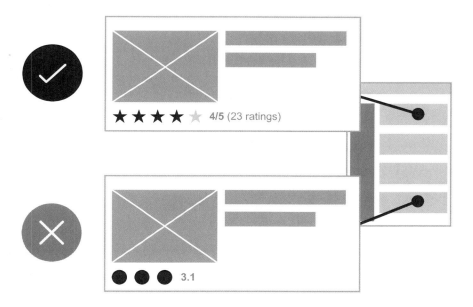

★ ★ ★ ★ ☆ **4/5** (23 ratings)

● ● ● 3.1

INDICATE PRODUCT VARIATIONS

If a product comes in a few different options—colours/ material/finish are examples—then you should show this to users on the search results. For example, users who are in the market for a blue sweater will be likely to pass by an image showing a red sweater unless there's a clear indicator that it is available in other colours.

The other option would be to have a separate product page for every variation, where they could all be viewed against each other on the search results. But be aware this could bloat your site with products to scroll through. I've also seen it cause confusion as users can end up comparing the same product against itself.

However if a variation in size or model means the product changes in price then it's usually a good idea to have a separate product page. This is better than displaying a range of prices on the search results, which makes comparison hard.

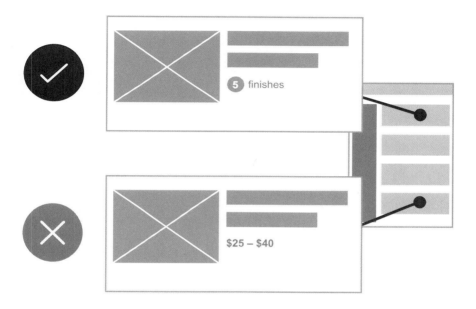

5 finishes

$25 – $40

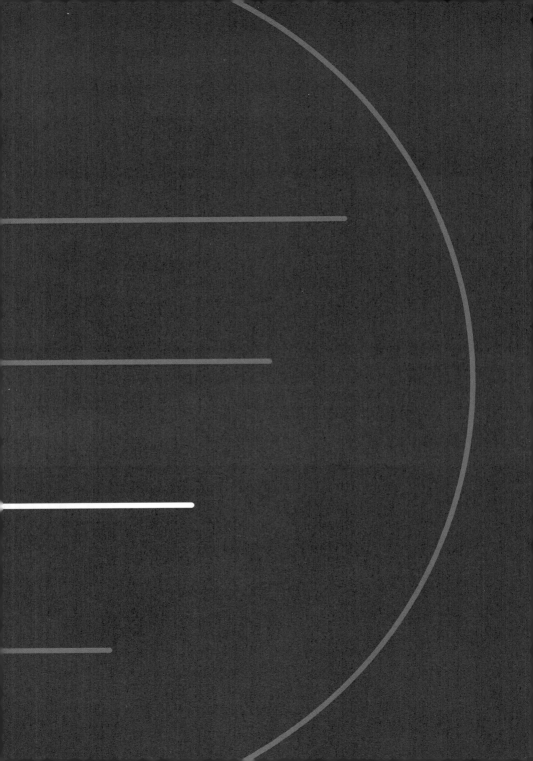

PRODUCT

The product page is where all the details about an individual product live. It's like the packaging, where the customer can't see the actual item but still wants a strong sense of both what it looks like and the specifications. Just like a boxed item, users can't touch a product online or see it with their own eyes. Your ecommerce sites might sell services or experiences but I class both as products, as they will have attributes to be described.

I would argue this is the most important step in the ecommerce funnel, because it has to convince users to buy. In fact the rest of the site can almost afford to be sloppy if you have great product pages, because these can be shared via social media, or found via Google searches.

When shopping for a product, a user tends to go through three different modes and the product page must solve for each of them. The modes are dreams, details, and fears. Not all products require all three of these to be met but the more expensive the product, the more they'll be needed.

— The **dreams** phase is the first stage and it is where the user needs to be made to feel excited about the offer on the table, namely the product itself. This stage may not apply to rudimentary, commodity items but for almost everything else it is important. The user must see themselves owning or experiencing the product and the benefits it will bring them. Things like imagery and descriptive copy help fulfil this need and make the user *want* it.

— The **details** follows the user's excitement about the product on offer and helps them get into thinking about the realities of making the purchase. Examples of this include: clothing coming in the right size; food being ethically sourced; hotels having a pool or gym; a car having the colour options you want. And for all products the most important detail is whether it comes in at the right price. This is where most of the decision making takes place and will determine whether this item is actually the right choice for the user.

— The **fears** step means allaying them and is more relevant the more money a user is spending. This is where they need to be reassured that the item is what it says it is and the website isn't lying to them. It's where a user will want to consult others' experiences to reassure themselves. Reviews play a big part here, as well as things like FAQs, shipping information (will I get something by a certain date?) and returns or cancellation policies.

This page must work for users who are ready to buy as well as those who want to study every detail before making a purchase. Almost every sector has users who won't buy without spending time fully understanding an item, so if you have information about it then make sure it's here. By organising it into clear sections you can also allow the confident buyers to scan quickly through.

This page is also a chance to show the most personality. It's where the product needs to come to life, so it can be less prescriptive than functional pages like search and checkout. Take these tips and build on them to create something a bit more special.

START WITH GREAT IMAGES

Imagery is one of the most important parts of the ecommerce process, particularly on the product page. Users can't see your product in real life or reach out and touch it (at least not yet anyway), so the imagery has a lot of heavy lifting to do. I've lost count of the number of user tests I've watched where users have got excited about looking through lots of photos. It should be the first thing they see on the page, to give them reason to look through the details.

Your imagery should feature consistently styled photography, and could also involve video. Even just a short clip of video can get across a lot more information than the best photo, especially for products where scale and fit are important to understand. Photos or videos with humans present really help add context and make something more real.

If you're selling experiences or something less physical, imagery can still be important to show the benefit of the service. For example if you're selling cheese tasting, the product isn't lumps of cheese but people gathered together enjoying themselves and learning. Don't fall for convenience and just put up the first pictures you can get your hands on. Put some effort into your styling and have a look you can own; it will help you stand out from your competitors.

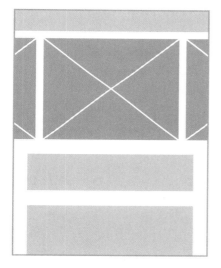

MAKE IT EASY TO BUY

This should go without saying but it's surprising how this isn't always done: the clearest action on a product page should be to buy that product (or add to basket). If you've got the user this far and interested, they shouldn't have to guess at how to give you their money. This page has one primary goal so help the user reach it.

The action should be a button and it should stand out, in a colour that is used sparingly elsewhere on the site. Don't blend it in, don't make the wording unclear, don't prioritise other actions on the page (like add to a wish list). It should be unmissable so it doesn't need to follow the user around the page (see **page 92**).

Avoid ever greying out this button, even if you want users to do something like select a size first, as they're likely to think they can't buy it. If they click the button without selecting a required size, you should pop up the size selector with an explaining message. When something actually is out of stock, you could replace it with a link to a contact form so they can ask to be informed when it is available again.

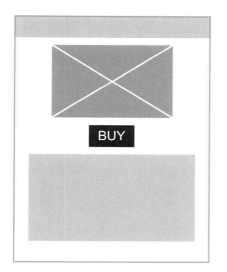

BUY

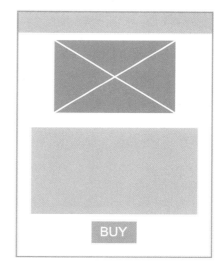

BUY

HAVE ALTERNATIVES TO PURCHASE

The ecommerce funnel can cause users to end up in dead-ends as even if users love a product they may not be ready to buy yet (particularly if it's an expensive product or one that requires other opinions before purchase). Rather than giving users a binary choice between buying or leaving the site altogether, consider having a softer secondary option.

This is where things like wish lists come into their own. Perhaps the user is still in the research phase, in which case being able to add items to a list for later is helpful. It's also great for you as it's a solid reason to ask for their email address, which means you can remind them to return later.

Another good secondary option is an enquiry form. This way if the user is uncertain about buying or has further questions, you give them a place where they can ask for help. This enquiry could then lead to a conversion over email or phone at a later date. If you have a phone number, put this near the buy button to be helpful for those users who are in a rush and need instant help.

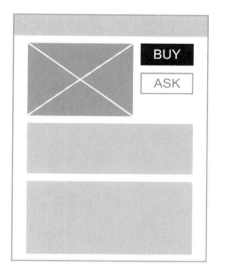

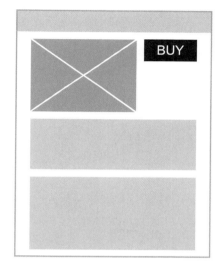

PRODUCT

BE CLEAR WHAT BIG PRICES MEAN

There are so many ways products can be priced, that if you aren't completely clear about how the pricing works users will often end up confused. This confusion is particularly prevalent with holidays and experiences, where users have their own expectations of how things should be priced depending on the size of the group they are used to booking for.

I've watched user tests of a holiday site where they just displayed a single 'from' price, which meant different users thought this was a total, a price per person, or a price per day. The site even put a price 'per guest per day' underneath the main price to help it seem good value but this led some users to think the big total was a flat rate and the smaller amount below was an additional cost.

If there's room for ambiguity then you can guarantee some users will get muddled, which could cost you trust and sales. Take the space to make sure you carefully describe what prices mean—at this stage of the journey the user won't want you to be vague.

$950 trip price
+ $150 per extra person
+ $400 room upgrade
+ $50 arrival drinks

$950 – $1550

DON'T HIDE IMAGE GALLERIES

If you have a load of images of your product that you want your users to see, the best place for them is an in-page carousel. This way a user just needs to tap a left or right arrow to find more. It's especially good if you can show a bit of the next and previous images to make it clear there are more in the carousel.

I've watched plenty of user tests of pages where the images are either thumbnails that need to be clicked to be viewed bigger, or a teaser image for a full pop-up gallery. In both cases the majority of users just scroll on past. A big carousel is much less likely to be missed and if the images are good quality then people will be highly engaged.

This matters because often images are the most important tool you have to sell a product and I've watched lots of users get excited when browsing through good ones. Make sure your pictures are being seen.

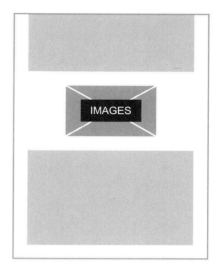

GIVE DETAIL IN
DIFFERENT FORMS

Any information available about a product should be on the product page. Give users as much as you can to help them feel confident about purchasing. Not all users will read it but some need to learn everything they can before they feel comfortable buying, so there's a benefit to it being there.

Examples of such information are descriptions, size guides, shipping details, dimensions, features, performance statistics, FAQs, even how-to videos. If you're selling complex, expensive things like trips there can be huge amounts of information to show like itineraries, room pricing, and package options. If you're selling simple, cheaper things which come with very little information, invest in some custom copy to make yours stand out against the competition.

Of course it shouldn't just be presented to the user in a block of text but should be broken up into relevant sections. You should utilise sub-headings, bullet points, tabs, tables, video, etc to make the details easier to consume.

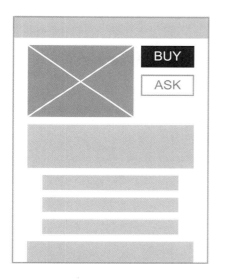

BUY

ASK

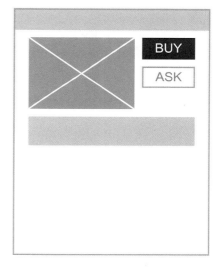

BUY

ASK

TIE YOUR PRODUCT TO YOUR USP

To go the extra mile and really get your product information working hard you should make sure there is a clear relationship to your brand or USP. This is that key difference you established on the landing page to explain why people should care about your store (see page 20).

This way if you're selling an item that can be purchased elsewhere you get to explain why the user should buy it from you rather than anyone else. Or if it is a unique item then you can remind the user of this and what makes it so different and special.

I've seen this done in plenty of ways, either through copy, video, or even infographics. It's a chance to both drive home your differentiator and to reach users who haven't seen it before, as they may have arrived direct on the product page.

How this is different

Product facts

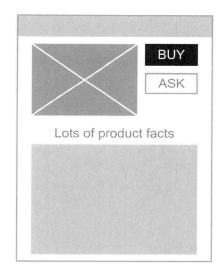

Lots of product facts

MAKE REVIEWS USEFUL

Where possible you should have reviews of your products for users to browse through. They're a known conversion improver and there are types of user who won't buy without digging through them.

Most importantly these reviews should be helpful to your target audience. Don't just blitz them with a series of five star ratings and one-liner reviews. These ratings can be quite subjective (what one person calls a four star, someone else might call three) and are less important than the content of the reviews themselves. Help users find reviews that are relevant to them.

You can do this by creating sections in each review, perhaps for product quality, size feedback, shipping feedback, etc. Or you can gather information from your users and display this to help people identify relevant reviews. Booking.com tells users the type of trip the reviewing guest was on (e.g. business or leisure) and their group type (e.g. couple or family). Equally tools site Screwfix tells users if the reviewer is a tradesman, which helps them know if their opinion is based on trade experience.

Reviews from people like you (3)

★ ★ ★ ★ ☆

★ ★ ★ ★ ★

All reviews (45)

★ ★ ★ ★ ☆

★ ★ ★ ★ ★

★ ★ ★ ☆ ☆

NO REVIEWS? GO TRANSPARENT

Whilst reviews are great, they aren't always possible for every site. For starters it can be a lot of work to set up a decent review collection system and in other cases it may not be a fit for the brand (high fashion and luxury sites tend not to go down this route). However if you don't have them, you can still meet the important requirement of building trust with the user by offering a form of transparency.

One option is to use social media to show how people are using the product. An Instagram feed of home-shot photos of your product in people's lives is a nice counterpoint to the slick brand photography.

Another option is to use copy to write truthfully in a section away from the sales description. Perhaps it's a few honest bullet points on things the user should know. For example, clearly stating 'this product should only be used by experts' helps them see you're not trying to rip them off. Or a short FAQs section, where you can tackle known questions and issues that previous customers have had.

"SHOW YOU'RE NOT TRYING TO RIP USERS OFF"

FINISH ON RELEVANT RELATED ITEMS

Related items are a section on most product pages, but some are better than others. They're good to have because if a user looks through all the information on a product and decides it isn't for them, you want to give them other options.

Related items should be relevant (not just a list of things you want to promote) and they should explain to the user *why* they are relevant. Don't just put a lazy title like 'related products' or 'things you might like'. Instead tell the user what makes them interesting, such as 'similar properties' or 'complementary pieces we've chosen'. Amazon have been the masters of this with three sets of related items per product page. It can veer into cross-selling, which is covered further on **page 94**.

Each related item is like a mini search listing, and should have an image, a title, and a price to help the user decide if it's right for them. It doesn't have to go into as much detail as search but each product needs some context.

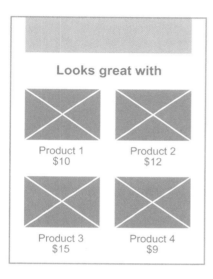

Looks great with

Product 1
$10

Product 2
$12

Product 3
$15

Product 4
$9

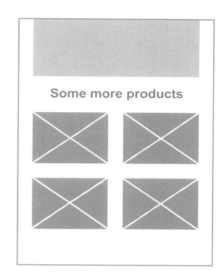

Some more products

CAREFUL WITH STICKY NAVIGATION

Some product pages can end up being very long with all the details you have to tell users. To prevent lots of scrolling you might be tempted to give them links to jump around the page on a 'sticky' navigation that follows the user as they scroll. Additionally you might feel the need to have a 'buy' button that follows them around so they just can't miss it.

However with most ecommerce sites now getting the majority of their traffic from mobile devices these can cause problems. For starters they can take up a lot of screen real estate on already-small screens. I measured a typical site with a sticky navigation at the top and bottom, which reduced the available area by 28%.

In-page navigation jumps users around with a lack of context and can disorientate users, and cause them think they're actually moving between different pages. This is exacerbated by having less screen space on mobile and can confuse their mental model of your site.

Scrolling, on the other hand, is the easiest interaction on the web. It's low cost and doesn't come with the fear of not knowing what will happen when you click a link. It's also a very precise way to position yourself on the page on touch screens.

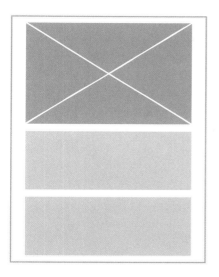

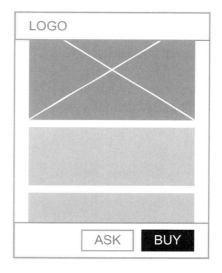

ASK BUY

THE RIGHT CROSS-SELL

Cross-selling or up-selling (or whatever you want to call offering more products) can appear at various points in the ecommerce funnel and it can be a powerful option to boost sales. There are a few approaches for doing so and you should consider which makes most sense for your store as it should be done in a way that doesn't cause users frustration.

If you're selling expensive products and the average order is around one item then you can consider putting up a whole page to offer users relevant additional products. This could appear after they've added something to a basket and as they're likely to only see it once, users should tolerate it or even find it useful.

If users are likely to be adding multiple things to their basket then this extra step would quickly get frustrating so consider making the offer on the product page (if you have bespoke offers per item) or only showing it on the basket screen itself (if it is a general promotion that applies across all purchases). You might even consider putting an up-sell right at the end of the checkout flow, as they are most committed to you at this stage and you have all the information to immediately take payment again.

"THIS CAN BE A POWERFUL OPTION TO BOOST SALES"

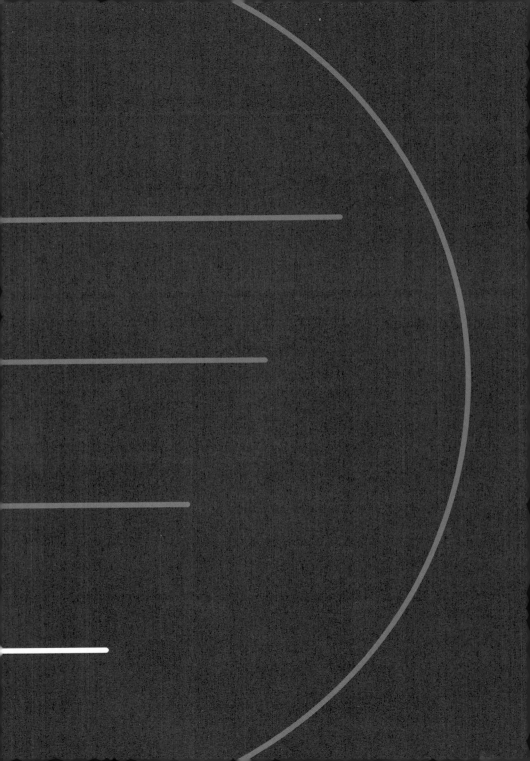

CHECKOUT

Now we come to the sharp end of the ecommerce funnel. The user has shown they are very keen on what you're selling and want to make a purchase, so this is the functional step of getting the requisite information to make that happen. It's often the most formulaic part of the site and an area where you can find a lot of design advice. Despite this, mistakes still get made: according to ecommerce specialists the Baymard Institute, 67% of sites studied in 2016 make usability errors here.

There are really only four potential sections to a checkout flow and you may not need all of them—certainly the flow shouldn't need to be any bigger than four pages. These are: product customisations; delivery information; billing information; and payment details.

— **Product customisations** tend to only exist when buying real life experiences, and they could be arrival times for hotel stays, seat selections for trains and planes, or booking additional services. These should come first, as they are likely to relate to the product page that the user has just been looking at. It's also a chance to ease the user into the checkout flow and get them to build their commitment to the act of paying.

— **Delivery information** is obviously a step that is only required if you will be dispatching items to customers. It's the next most important as it could alter the price and you want to allow users to see this soon rather than spring it on them at the end. If they're keen to get something by a certain date they'll want to find out early on if this is possible. At this stage you need an address and possibly a phone number for delivery drivers to contact.

— Now we move onto **billing information**, which is going to be required by all sites. These are the essentials required to process a payment by most payment providers and they usually entail a name and address (you can speed this up by asking the user if it's the same as the delivery one). You should ask for an email address by this point so you can contact them about their order—and if it's a digital product, this will form the delivery mechanism.

— Finally we reach the **payment details**, a step every flow will have. This usually comes last because it involves a third party and you'll want to be sure you've collected everything you need first before sending user's details over to them. Virtually every site will use a third party to process their payments even if it's hidden from the user. At this point the user enters their all-important card details.

The linear nature of a checkout flow means there's a clear metric as to whether something has succeeded or not and makes it the easiest to test. You should have a funnel measuring how successful these steps are and the one with the lowest conversion is your first port of call to improve.

The checkout flow is one step in the ecommerce chain whose days may be numbered—certainly in the sense of having a custom one for every different store. With the convenience of payment wallets on mobile like Apple Pay, it will be much easier to just pay with a fingerprint. If you're going to continue to get those valuable customer details, then your checkout will have to be super-smooth to compete against the massive convenience of single-tap payments.

Checkout flows are a form-filling exercise and generally users find this dull and are prone to making mistakes. Whatever you can do to make this easier or more convenient is valuable here. All these tips are based around doing that.

REDUCE THE LINKS

You've probably noticed when you enter other online checkout flows it feels like you're in a different version of the site. It is usually much more stripped back. The header loses a lot of its links, the site-wide navigation disappears, and the footer links go, to be replaced with just basic copyright and legal notes.

The links should be reduced because you don't want users getting distracted when they're in the checkout flow. This is a key point of the journey where they've expressed a strong interest in buying, so make it as easy as possible for them to do that. If they suddenly spot a new product on the navigation they may click it, read about this new product, compare it to one on another site, and forget to convert with you.

People ask if there should be *any* links at all, and some checkout flows have a few but I tend to design them with none (other than ones to other checkout steps). This includes removing the link to the homepage from the logo. It just makes things clearer and more focussed. If the user wants to leave there's always a browser back button or they can close the window altogether.

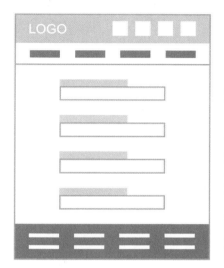

SHOW THE NUMBER OF STEPS

One thing you should show in your checkout header is an indication of how long the checkout flow will take users to complete. Generally this is shown in how many steps or pages there are until the order is placed.

This indicator gives users a rough guide to the length of the process. Just like waiting times feel shorter when you can see how long it will take, giving users an indication of the length of the flow makes them much more likely to complete. Each step feels more manageable this way and the user gets the reward of a mini-goal when they complete each page.

In terms of UI design, you'll need three link styles for the step indicators: one showing that a user has completed a step; one showing that a user is on a step; and one showing that a step is still to come. Don't be tempted to reduce it to fewer styles as I've seen this confuse users. You should allow users to move back to completed steps in the flow, either via the links or through the browser back button.

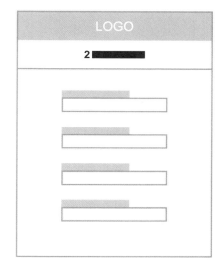

A SINGLE COLUMN

You should make sure your checkout flow forms are
incredibly easy to fill in. One of the best ways to do this
is to have the form be a single column, which helps the
user easily see what they have to do. A single direction
of focus helps the form itself act as a progress bar, as the
user should easily be able to see what they have and haven't
filled in, and where they're up to on the page. There's no
extra dimension of jumping across columns going left
to right as well.

Not only should there not be multiple form columns but it
makes life even easier if there's no content to the left or right
at all. Excess content (even if it doesn't require filling in) can
distract users from the main task at hand. One of the best
improvements to checkout conversion I made to a checkout
flow in the past involved getting rid of the order information
running down the right side and having just the form.

The best way to work is to design it for mobile first and then
centre that layout on a desktop (maybe with slightly wider fields).
All fields should run vertically down the page, with no fields next
to each other (like first name and last name) and with the field
labels above rather than to the left.

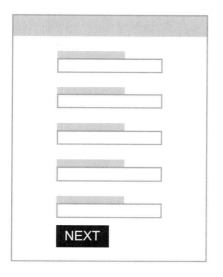

NEXT

NEXT

ALLOW GUEST CHECKOUT

One of the biggest barriers to checkout completion is asking your users to sign up or create an account before checking out. It adds that extra bit of hassle and thought to someone's journey: "Do I need to? Shall I just go to another site I'm already registered with?". Asking for passwords is getting in the way, when at this point you should be getting out of the way and making it easy for them to part with their cash.

Even if you're a site where the user will need an account to log back in later—like an accommodation or transport provider—you still don't have to get the user to create a password up front. And that's the only field difference for new members: a password. You can get them to create it at the end of the process, when their order is placed, or you can create them an account with their email address and email them a password reset later.

Be smart about it: the user didn't come to register for your site, they came to buy your product or service. Give them that before asking for more.

Checkout as guest

Log in

Register

Log in

AVOID UNNECESSARY FIELDS

There's a theme to the content in this section and it's this: keep things simple. Only ask for exactly what you need from the user to complete the transaction.

Don't ask for phone numbers unless you will actually call them; don't ask for gender unless it's relevant; don't ask for date of birth unless there's a legal requirement to. Every extra field is added complexity, more typing that's required, and more chances for errors.

If you're selling digital products (audio, video, ebooks) then the only delivery information you'll need is an email address to accompany the payment details. This can be done in four fields. Or if they're on a mobile, you could use their camera to photograph the card with a tool like card.io to reduce the amount of fiddly mobile keyboard effort needed.

Name

[   ]

Email

[   ]

NEXT

Name

[   ]

Email

[   ]

How did you find us?

[   ]

Where else do you shop?

[   ]

NEXT

KEEP CTAS THE SAME

Calls To Action (CTAs) have already been covered as an important part of landing pages (see page 24) and product pages (see page 74). And guess what? They're also an important part of your checkout flow. Especially as they're going to appear a few times on a multi-step checkout.

As well as following the other rules, such as being in a clear contrast colour to the rest of the page, if you've got a CTA on each step they should look and read the same. That means not changing the wording for each step of a checkout flow, as it requires extra thought from the user to interpret what it does.

Think of your CTAs as training the user into what to expect: if the first two steps use the word 'Next' or 'Continue' you should keep that the same on the third, as you've built the expectation that this will take them forward in the process. Changing it to say 'Pay' or adding extra copy underneath to reassure actually often does the opposite and causes some users to question rather than act instinctively. I've pushed up the conversion of a checkout step by 25% by changing a differing CTA to match with the others in the flow.

The exception is if you're sending users to another site to pay. This is something you should make clear so they aren't shocked when it happens.

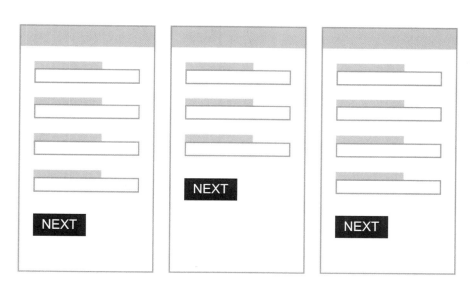

1 **2** **3**

CONSIDER PAYPAL AND WALLETS

I've watched many user tests where the users have been happy to see PayPal as an option in the checkout flow, hearing them say comments like "I much prefer the option of using PayPal" and "my husband is very security conscious and will only pay using PayPal". The fees can be pretty expensive on the seller side so it's not always the best option for the business but some users will be much happier when they see the chance to have additional protection. Especially if your site is new or relatively unknown.

There are now other payment wallets than PayPal coming to the fore, some of them tightly integrated with the user's hardware. At the time of writing, Apple Pay has recently been enabled for use within browsers. If you want to make it easy for mobile users to convert, it makes sense to support this.

Using a payment wallet means that the user has already supplied their payment information, personal details, and address, so a simple tap (in the case of Apple Pay) can transmit all of that to your site. This could even save you creating large parts of the checkout flow altogether. Of course, until the majority of users embrace these systems you'll have to offer a standard flow too, but by having payment wallets as additional checkout options you'll learn your users' preferences.

" THIS COULD SAVE YOU CREATING LARGE PARTS OF THE CHECKOUT FLOW "

SUBTLE PROMO CODE FIELDS

Whether they are on your basket or in the checkout, don't make your promo code fields too obvious. You can be guaranteed that if you make it a dominant field or it interrupts the user's flow, then it will cause them to try Googling for a discount code. You may not mind that they use a discount but the action of going off to search for one could cause them to get distracted and not return to their purchase.

It's better to place it as a secondary action on the screen, at the bottom or slightly out the way. It should be somewhere it can be found if you have a code and are looking for it but not somewhere that will trigger everyone to go searching. Requiring the user to click or tap to reveal the field can also help make it more subtle.

In the flow, promo code fields should appear on your basket or early in the checkout if your site doesn't have a full basket page. This is because you want users to know they can use their discount if they have one. If it's hidden away on the last step then some users will assume there isn't the option and not convert at all.

NEXT

▼ Promo code?

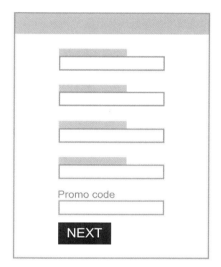

Promo code

NEXT

ALL THE DELIVERY INFORMATION

If you're delivering products to your users then there's some key information you should supply. From research I've carried out with ecommerce users I established three elements that make an ideal delivery message. When users saw all of these present they were more likely to be satisfied and make a purchase. It may not be technically possible for you to provide these to your users, but for each delivery option that you offer you should show three things:

— The date or time the product will be dispatched. If you dispatch items on the same day as the order then it's worth stating this, as seeing the word 'today' comes across as prompt and reassuring. If the dispatch date is further away then that is equally worth telling people up front so they can make an informed decision.
— The date they will receive the item. This is obviously the most important element to the user, especially if they have to be around to collect it, and there should be at least an estimate of this stated. Even better is a guaranteed delivery date or time if you can.
— The cost of the delivery. Not surprisingly people are going to want to know how much their choice of delivery method will cost. If you offer next day delivery be clear which option this applies to, and that it's probably not going to be the free delivery you may promote elsewhere.

This kind of information should certainly live in the checkout and likely in the shopping basket too. In a lot of cases it is helpful to have in a condensed form (perhaps not with all the options) on the product page to help a user know if it's worth progressing further with buying.

Delivery

Order in next **3 hours** for dispatch today

Standard delivery Free | Receive by Saturday
Express delivery £10 | Receive by Thursday

Delivery

Standard delivery – Free
Express delivery – £10

UNDERSTAND YOUR PAYMENT PROVIDER

When you take money from customers you will need a partner service who deals with processing the payments. These include Braintree, Adyen, Global Collect, Stripe, etc. Not all payment providers are created equal though, so it's worth understanding what yours offers and what their limitations are, as it can affect UX decisions.

There are several questions you should ask and work out with your developers. Does the provider require information to be collected first about the payee and then passed onto them? This could define what order steps need to come in. Do you have full control over the styling of the form fields, or will they be fixed by the payment provider? This could hamper how consistent you keep your experience. Will they use pop-ups/iframes/redirects to take the user to the payment step? This isn't ideal and can really break up a smooth checkout process.

Put simply, it comes down to control. How much do they allow you to completely customise the experience to your site and how much do they mandate for you. Work this out early before it scuppers any plans you may have.

"WORK *THIS* OUT EARLY BEFORE *IT* SCUPPERS *YOUR* PLANS"

BASIC FORM USABILITY

Checkout flows are essentially a form filling exercise and no-one finds that particularly enjoyable. It's worth learning from the wealth of usability knowledge that has been built up around designing effective forms. Here are three tips you should certainly follow:

1. Put labels above—avoid having your field label sit on the left of the field itself as this layout can break on smaller screens and it's not always easy to see the relationship if the gap gets too wide. Much better is to have the label sit above the field, where the relationship is much clearer and it will work across all devices.

2. Show errors inline (after filling out)—a good error message is shown on the field itself so the user can instantly see where they went wrong, and not have to scan the page to discover the offending item. The error message shouldn't show up while the user is still typing however, which is annoying and can cause them to think they're wrong when they just haven't finished typing.

3. Avoid placeholders—placeholder text that sits inside a field has grown in popularity as designers look for ways to streamline their designs and save space. It can work for very small forms but on longer things like checkout flows it can make fields look filled out when they haven't been. It's also a good idea to put any help text above the field rather than in it, because as soon as the user starts typing that help disappears.

EMAIL

```
[                    ]
```

1

EMAIL
```
[                    ]
```

EMAIL
```
[ nameemail.com ]
```

Please check this is a valid email

2

EMAIL
```
[ name| ]
```

Please check this is a valid email

EMAIL
Enter your work email
```
[                    ]
```

3

EMAIL
```
[ Enter your work email ]
```

MORE FORM USABILITY

Here are a few more tips on form design, that deal with some of the more subtle things you should consider:

1. Avoid dropdowns where possible—the dropdown or select field is a fiddly thing but it can be tempting just to throw them in when you have multiple options you want users to choose from. However, when a list of options is small (fewer than about six) you should break them out into a set of radio buttons. This way the user can easily see all the options available and choose with a single click or tap (it's particularly friendly for mobile), avoiding the extra click/tap to open the menu. For long lists the dropdown will probably still be required.

2. Nudge with field size—the size that you set your fields to can help users see how much text they are expected to enter in them. If it's a post or zip code you can help users realise they only need to enter a few characters by making it smaller than a phone number field. Equally if you need to use a text area for a user message then the overall size of that will help indicate how many lines are expected of them.

3. Use autocomplete—make sure you utilise the browser autocomplete feature (this is more of a developer tip but one you should still take advantage of). If a user has it enabled it can save them typing in their name, email, phone number, and address—all things they're likely to have entered in the browser many times before. This is particularly useful for mobile devices as typing is harder on small screens so anything you can do to reduce it will be appreciated.

CARD TYPE

VISA | Mastercard | AMEX

1

CARD TYPE

Please choose ▼

POST CODE

2

POST CODE

EMAIL

n|

first.lastname@email.com

3

EMAIL

first.lastname@email.com

✓ ✕

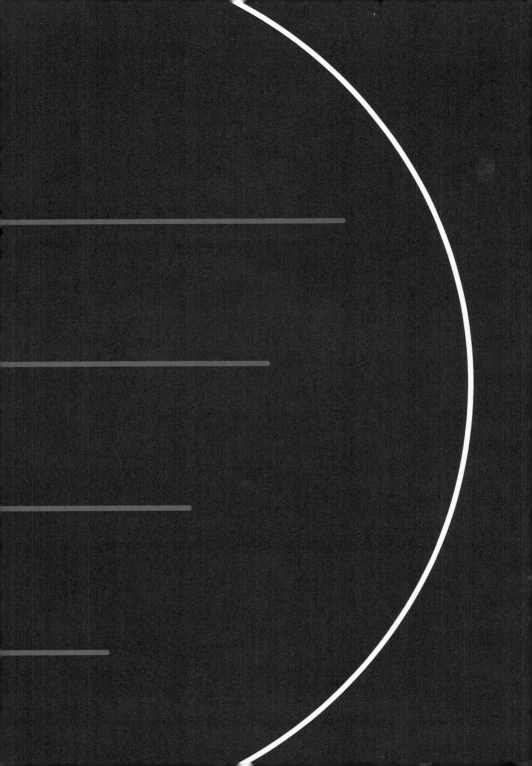

MORE

This section of the book is here for those tips that don't fit into the main categories of the ecommerce funnel steps. These extra tips could be described as falling into three categories: site-wide considerations, 'about' pages, or content pages.

— The site-wide considerations are things that can potentially apply to every step in the flow and are worth establishing for your site to maintain consistency.

— 'About' pages or information pages are not directly sales related but do offer a space to give more detail about the company, a product or a line of products. Some sites stop at a standard 'about us' page but more can be done to explain things to your users.

— Content-led ecommerce brands will generate their own editorial as an approach to inbound marketing and attracting users to visit. People can treat this as a completely separate section but in truth it's usually just a layer on top of a standard ecommerce funnel and an alternative form of landing page.

This section covers seven of the most important pieces of advice for helping the whole of your ecommerce website tick along nicely.

ONE WAY ACCESS
VIA CONTENT

The ecommerce funnel is a fairly simple affair but you might want to start building out additional content to capture your users' interest. Perhaps you're selling something very expensive that people won't buy often, so you want to build their trust first. Maybe an editorial approach is a key part of your USP and a chance to explore your distinctive voice and grow your brand.

There are a couple of UX rules to effectively utilising this attention. The first is to make sure these content pages have clear links through to the products and category pages. Your content should be related to what you sell (even if it isn't specifically about that) and it should be obvious where to find your products. Not all users will be interested in buying but make it easy for those that are.

The second rule is to not put links to content on the product pages. The process should be a one-way street sending people from content through to shop. You don't want intriguing content cannibalising users' interest and distracting them away from the main focus of the product page, which is to sell. It dilutes the purpose of the page. If there's helpful information in your content then integrate it further up the ecommerce funnel, on landing pages, or perhaps search.

SHOP

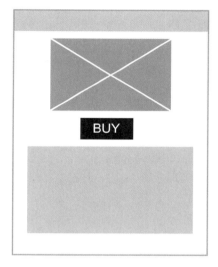

BUY

KEEP INFO PAGES PUNCHY

It can be a good idea to have an information or 'about' page for certain product lines or even the whole site brand itself, especially if it is a new company or something that needs explanation. It is effectively a continuation of the principle of 'telling users why you're different' (see page 20) and the page should focus on no more than three key reasons.

Use it as a chance to go into detail on exactly why your process, product, or service is so much better than the competition. By keeping it to three important differences you make it more likely that the user will remember them. Additional things can be summarised as bullet points at the bottom of the page but you're probably scraping the barrel by this point.

Whilst this is a chance to go into detail, you should illustrate with imagery and break the text up into short, scannable sections as people don't tend to read long blocks of copy, especially when they're in shopping mode (not newspaper reading mode).

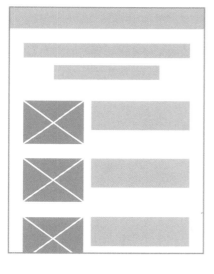

LUXURY IS IN
THE VISUALS

The most obvious difference between a high-end site selling expensive products and a site selling more commodity products, is really in the visual design. The difference in typefaces, colours, white space, and quality of imagery can be understood at a glance. Consciously or not, the surface design matters to users and should be congruent with the products available for sale. So if you're aiming to charge users a lot, then the design of the website had better back this up.

High-end sites generally go for only one or two typefaces, with only a few variations in size and style (often with minimal use of bold and italics). The colour palette is usually fairly restrained and kept to muted colours, or even just black and white with one accent colour. White space tends to be used liberally to give that feeling of luxury and to show the content isn't packed in or constrained. Finally the imagery will be high quality, and given centre-stage.

Of course there are other things in the UX that count towards a high quality experience, like page loading speeds and a lack of unnecessary extra steps in the user journey. Even with good UX, users will judge you quickest by how the visual design looks.

"
CONSCIOUSLY
OR
NOT,
THE
SURFACE
DESIGN
MATTERS
TO
USERS
"

HAVE CONTACTS
IN THE HEADER

Don't make it hard for users to contact you. You want to make it clear how users can contact a human—failing to do so risks your sales. This contact method can be email or phone but either way it's important to give users this option.

People can run into issues on your site on any page, and whether they are struggling to find their way around or have a pressing question about a product, you should make it easy to get in touch wherever they are. Thus as a result, the best place to put your key contact details is in the header. If you have a staffed phone line, it's definitely a positive to show this off as it builds trust and helps less-confident web users see there is a safety net.

You may lack the header space on mobile so putting it at the top of the footer is a good idea too. This way it's always on every page. Mobile users will be holding a device that can make phone calls so make the number a telephone link to enable them to call with a tap.

0800 123 4567
Call 8am – 8pm | Live chat

Contact us

NAVIGATION TO REFLECT POPULARITY

If you have a site with hundreds of products and tens of categories, how do you arrange this information? Especially when you are likely to have limited space on your navigation menus. The answer is to prioritise what is popular.

You can determine what is popular by keeping track of your web analytics as well as your sales. If you have some pretty niche product areas that don't attract many users or purchases then don't feel the need to put them on your navigation. Top level navigations should have no more than about seven options and lists below that should stick to 10-15 items.

Don't feel the need to make every category immediately visible, because every option in a list is an extra bit of information for users to comprehend and make a decision about. It's not about reflecting every single thing on your site, it's about making it easy for the majority of users to find the things they most often want. Of course this might change over time so keep up to date with how your product lines are evolving and how user behaviour changes with that.

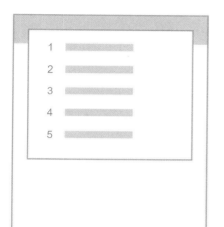

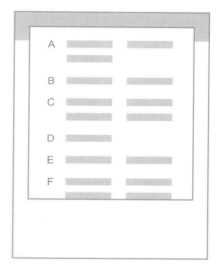

LET USERS EDIT THEIR COUNTRY & CURRENCY

This tip only applies if you're selling to different countries although it isn't to do with languages or translation: you should allow the user to set which country they are in and ideally which currency they want to shop in.

These customisations increase the chance that the user will convert. It means the user can feel confident that their country is supported by the store and any orders will reach them, and that they will also be quoted the right taxes and shipping. Users seeing prices in their native currency are much more likely to feel at home with what's on offer and don't have to keep doing conversion sums to work out if they can afford something. It's trivial for a machine to do this task so don't put it upon your users.

You can automatically detect where users are coming from through their IP address but you should allow the user to specify this themselves too. IP detection isn't always accurate and there can be cases where users are abroad but intend to order to their home country.

Headers and footers are good places to provide this link to set the country and currency. I like to bring up the options in a modal window, so the user can stay on their page and not break their journey.

Country

United Kingdom ▼

Currency

€ EUR ▼

Country

United Kingdom

Currency

£ GBP

KNOW YOUR CMS

The choice of Content Management System (CMS) governs many of the limitations on what can be achieved in any ecommerce site. Many (though not all) websites are built using one as it can save a lot of time when updating. This is particularly true for ecommerce sites, which others have built many times before.

If you have a custom-built site then anything should be possible but if you use a CMS then it is worth understanding how it is structured and what can be achieved with it. It will often affect how search is displayed and the ability to customise filters. It can also influence what order the checkout process comes and how basket functionality works, including things like promo codes and vouchers.

Another thing that forms a part of the design of your site but is often overlooked, is the URL structure. Does your CMS allow for you to identify page types, categories, and product names from the URL? Or is it all just a messy query string? If you can design the URLs then you can create a structure that is scalable and makes it easy to identify different pages in web analytics tools.

Knowing the tools and the medium you work in is important for any designer. Get a developer to help you understand if it all gets a bit too technical.

"KNOWING THE TOOLS AND THE MEDIUM YOU WORK IN IS IMPORTANT"

GLOSSARY

Attention ratio

The ratio of all links on a page to the the most important link you want users to choose (which should always be one). A high ratio is usually a warning sign you have too much on your page.

Baymard Institute

A company who study ecommerce websites through usability tests. On **page 98** I reference research which can be found at http://baymard.com/blog/ecommerce-checkout-usability-report-and-benchmark

Bounce rate

The rate of web browsing sessions which result in the user leaving the site having only viewed one page. Expressed as a percentage.

Card.io

Code which enables users to photograph their credit card with their smart phone to save typing in the long card number. This functionality is built into many apps.

Carousel

An interactive element on a webpage which rotates through several different sets of images (often with text).

CMS

This stands for Content Management System and is where website administrators are able to edit the text and images on a website without needing to code.

Copy

Any kind of written content but often that which has been written for marketing purposes.

CTA

This stands for Call To Action and refers to the text that users must click or tap to complete an action. This text often lives on a button.

Dynamically update

A website which updates with new content without the user having to click a button to refresh the page.

Query string

The text which comes after a '?' In a URL and tells the website what content it should be displaying on the page.

The fold

An imaginary line on a website marked out by the height of your browser window, which obviously varies by device. Elements are then said to be either above or below the fold.

Thumbnails

Small images which tend to link to full-size versions of the same images.

USP

This stands for Unique Selling Point and is a marketing term for what makes your product special and different.

AFTERWORD

Thanks for reading! I hope you found it useful and have found a few new tips for your next project. With a bit of luck this will continue to be something you can return to in future.

I'd love to hear your feedback on this book itself and whether it has been useful in your design work. Either email me on matt@mattish.com or fill out the quick form on my site at the link below. Alternatively you can drop me a tweet—I'm @ishmatt. I'm also open to running bespoke workshops on the content in this book.

The world of web design is always evolving and I'll probably come up with a few new tips to add further down the line. Any future ecommerce UX advice I write up will be made available on my site, and they will be free for those of you who have bought this book.

Simply go to **mattish.com/ecombonus** to sign up for infrequent email updates about new content. I've also got plans to produce more in the ecommerce design space, including adapting this material into an online course. I'll be sure to keep you in the loop about that too.

ACKNOWLEDGEMENTS

As ever my biggest thanks go to my partner Jen, for both being supportive of my ideas (even when they occasionally reach into weekends) and for being my keen-eyed editor. Her honesty, patience, and better grasp of English have made this a much better read.

A big thanks must also go to my good friend Nam, who has done a great job of designing this book and passing on his print expertise. You should definitely hire him—check out **nam-design.co.uk**.

Thank you to everyone who has attended one of my General Assembly ecommerce UX workshops, particularly the early ones. I've done 17 of them since 2013 and sharp student questioning has helped the content improve, and in turn shaped this book.

Finally, cheers to all the folks on my mailing list for engaging with my UX content every couple of weeks, especially those who filled out my ecommerce survey which helped me decide the scope of this book. You can join my growing band at **mattish.com/newsletter**.